The 1:1 Assistant's Guidebook

Practical Information for Learning Support Aides Working with Students with Autism

By: S. B. Linton
AutismClassroom.com

TABLE OF CONTENTS

WELCOME

Welcome to the 1:1 Assistant's Guidebook. Hopefully, this book can give you a good start for working with individuals with autism and intellectual disabilities. This was created to be an interactive book with spaces for you to fill in your thoughts, feelings and newly learned information. It is my hope that you find this book helpful and that you will want to recommend it to a friend, family member or co-worker working with a child with autism.

Thank you,

S. B. Linton

INFORMATION ABOUT AUTISM

Autism is becoming more and more prevalent in our society. Ten years ago 1 in 166 children were diagnosed with autism. Today, some researchers are saying that 1 in 88 children have some form of an autism spectrum disorder. More and more, there are news stories, websites and services related to working with individuals with autism. Autism is called a spectrum because you can find various ability levels, sensory needs, intellectual levels and social skills from people with autism. Individuals with autism are a very diverse group. For example, there are those with autism that have average to above average intellectual abilities and there are some individuals that have intellectual disabilities. In either case, an understanding of how to reach the students and effective teaching techniques are needed to help students to maximize their learning potential.

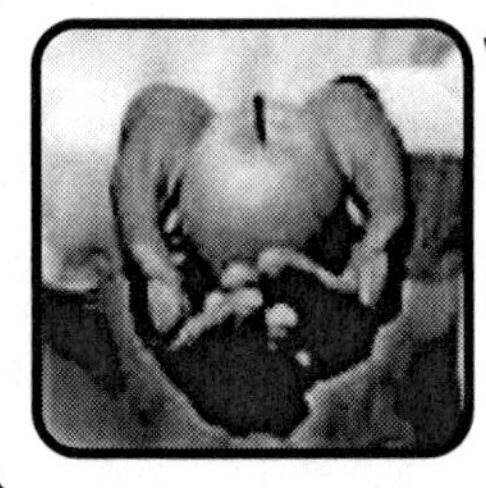

Write about your experience with individuals with autism.

What do you know about individuals with autism?

What are some things you hope to learn about teaching individuals with autism?

The Autism Society of America defines autism as a complex developmental disability that typically appears during the first three years of life and affects a person's ability to communicate and interact with others. Autism is defined by a certain set of behaviors and is a "spectrum disorder" that affects individuals differently and to varying degrees. To diagnose autism, a clinician may look for:

~ Qualitative impairments in social interaction.

~ Qualitative impairments in communication.

~ Restricted, repetitive and stereotyped patterns of behavior.

GENERAL CHARACTERISTICS

- All children are unique; no two people with autism have the exact same characteristics and no one person has all possible characteristics
- Strong visual learners (process information better by seeing, rather than by hearing alone)
- Restricted interests
- Resists changes in routine
- Uneven gross and fine motor skills
- Anxiety

SOCIAL CHARACTERISTICS

- Limited interest in social interaction; limited skills in social interaction
- Limited eye contact
- Difficulty with pragmatics and reading social cues
- Difficulty understanding sarcasm
- Difficulty understanding figures of speech such as "knock it off"
- Ritualistic play patterns (spinning, lining objects)
- Limited joint attention (attending to what others are attending to)

COMMUNICATION CHARACTERISTICS

- Uses gestures or pointing, rather than words
- May repeat words (Echolalia)
- May repeat lyrics (Echolalia)
- May repeat commercials (Echolalia)
- May repeat lines from movies or television (Echolalia)
- May repeat sounds (Echolalia)
- Atypical patterns of speech

SENSORY CHARACTERISTICS

- Avoidance response to being held or cuddled
- May seek a firm touch or weighted items
- May avoid or dislike a light touch
- May avoid or seek out scents
- Differences in visual responses
- May appear to be over-sensitive or under-sensitive to pain
- Stereotyped and repetitive mannerisms

BEHAVIORAL CHARACTERISTICS

- Inappropriate laughing or giggling
- Tantrums
- Crying/tantrum for no identifiable reason
- Over attachment to objects
- Atypical fear responses (too much or too little fear of everyday things)
- Over-active or under-active movement

LEARNING CHARACTERISTICS

- Performs better with visual supports (real objects, photos, etc.)
- Hands-on learning experiences needed
- Communication has to be taught
- Communication has to be reinforced
- Need educators to break tasks into smaller parts
- Benefits from short learning blocks with movement breaks

Like all of us, individuals with autism have things they are good at and things that are challenging to them. It would be helpful to you as a 1:1 educator to know and understand how some of these things may affect the person you are working with.

Strengths for some people with autism

- The ability to stick to routines
- A good visual memory when information can be seen instead of spoken
- The ability to think concretely and logically
- Exceptional memory
- Attention to detail
- Honesty
- Straightforwardness
- Intense focus on tasks that are interesting to the individual

Challenging areas for some people with autism

- Effectively and independently making social connections with others
- Being flexible with situations, and routines
- Self-Control when things become overwhelming
- Recognizing how behavior affects others
- Communication Skills (taking turns in a conversation, starting a conversation, staying on topic, etc.)
- Perspective Taking (taking other people's perspectives and understanding that others think differently than they might be thinking)
- Paying attention to the responses of others
- Reading the faces of others to gain information

Setting up the space is important for a number of reasons. First, the environment of a home or school can potentially be overwhelming to a child with autism due to the loud noises, intense scents, bright colors and unpredictability. We can try to make it easier for the child to be successful if we modify a few items in the setting. Secondly, research from the TEACCH (teacch.com) program in North Carolina, shows that by making consistent and focused environmental changes, you can greatly increase the independence of some children with autism. Finally, we know that an organized and structured space is helpful to all children, with or without autism.

IF YOU ARE WORKING IN THE <u>SCHOOL SETTING</u> YOU WILL WANT TO DO THE FOLLOWING THINGS:

- ✓ *Limit visual distractions such as items hanging from the walls*
- ✓ *Remove clutter from desk tops and counter tops*
- ✓ *Use furniture to your advantage by creating small nooks to work in*
- ✓ *Place work areas near blank walls and away from mirrors*
- ✓ *Use a work area near shelves to make it easier to store materials*
- ✓ *Use furniture that is the correct size for the student*
- ✓ *Label materials, toys and supplies with pictures or photos for non-readers and non-verbal students to encourage communication and build their vocabulary*

IF YOU ARE WORKING IN THE <u>HOME SETTING</u> YOU WILL WANT TO DO THE FOLLOWING THINGS:

- ✓ *Limit visual distractions when possible during work times*
- ✓ *Remove clutter from the area where you will do work*
- ✓ *Use furniture that is the correct size for the child*
- ✓ *Label materials with pictures to build vocabulary*
- ✓ *Set up a special workspace*
- ✓ *Create a play area where you can sit and play a table top game as well as play movement games*
- ✓ *Use calming colors like blues and greens*

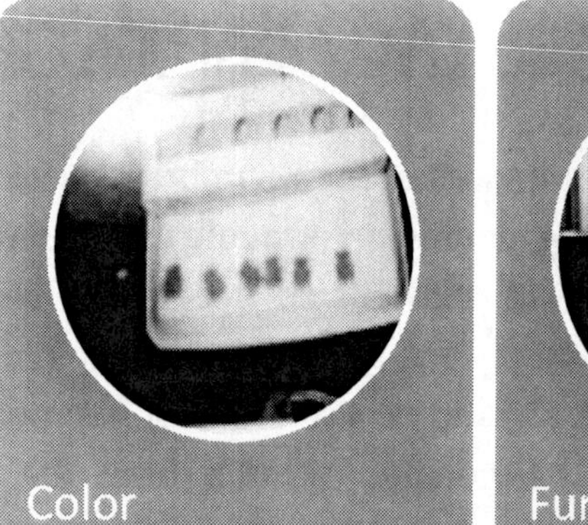

Color

- Blues and Greens are usually calming colors
- Reds, Yellows and Oranges may be alerting and painful to look at

Furniture

- The wrong size furniture could be distracting
- Use the furniture as dividers and boundaries for different areas of the room

Distractions

- Open window blinds and open doors can be distracting
- Plain fabric can be used to cover shelves or walls during work times

IDEAS FOR SETTING UP A **WORK SPACE** TO WORK ON SPECIFIC LEARNING OBJECTIVES:

- Find a large bin with a lid to store the materials inside.
- Use zippered baggies to create one labeled baggie for each objective. Use a permanent marker to write on the baggie.
- Store the materials for each objective in their own baggie.
- Create a "fun box" which has a variety of about 6 of the child's preferred, favorite items. The fun box will be most effective if the student is only allowed access to it during work times and not at other times.
- Use the fun box (for 30 seconds) after a correct response or after meaningful participation.

3 DATA COLLECTION

Data collection is the monitoring of student progress towards I.E.P. goals and learning objectives. Each child in Special Education has an Individualized Education Program or I.E.P. that highlights the individualized needs of the student. In order to track how well the student is meeting their learning objectives, data based on those goals and objectives must be collected. Various types of progress monitoring sheets are used to accomplish this. Each classroom team will use the data monitoring sheets that are most effective for them.

TYPES OF DATA

Frequency- number of times a behavior occurs

Duration- amount of time a behavior occurs

Latency- amount of time between the start of the opportunity and the start of the behavior

Percent- # of occurrences out of # of opportunities

Intensity- physical force or magnitude of the behavior

Time Sample- observation period divided into intervals

Permanent Product- the product the student creates or worksheet the student completes

Interval recording- recording the behavior in intervals (ex. every 10 minutes)

ABC Data- writing down the antecedent, behavior, and consequence for a particular behavior

Keeping records on progress is necessary due to a high emphasis on accountability in our education system. It will be important to know how progress in measured in the setting you work in. Some students you encounter will complete tasks independently. However, some may require prompts or cues to help them get the task correct. Many educators use a key for recording the type of prompts or cues needed to successfully complete a task. The most common types of prompts used are verbal prompts, gesture prompts, modeling prompts, physical prompts, positional prompts, and visual prompts.

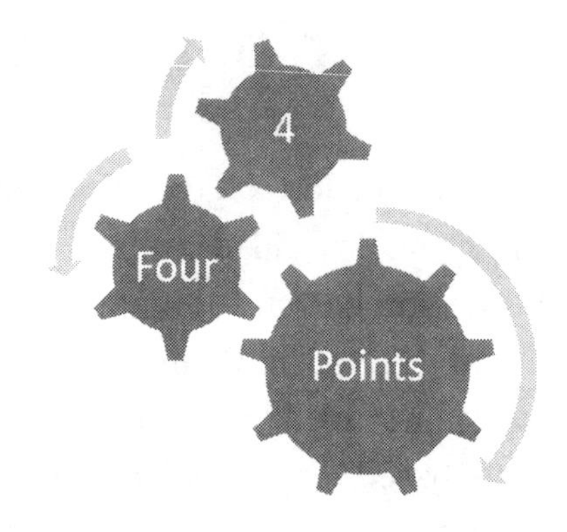

WHAT IS THIS?

Data collection is monitoring through the written tracking of student progress. Educators use pre-made forms or self-made forms to track student progress on learning objectives, IEP goals, curriculum standards and behavioral challenges.

WHAT DOES THIS MEAN?

Student progress must be tracked in order to know if the student is making gains, if the student is regressing, if the student is staying the same or if the students is making no progress.

WHY IS THIS IMPORTANT TO ME?

You might be asked to collect data related to the student's learning objectives or behavioral challenges. Additionally, you may want to know if your teaching methods are effective.

WHY IS THIS IMPORTANT TO THE STUDENT?

If the student is not making progress, then you will know that the teaching method is not working or the task is too difficult. You may have to break the task into smaller parts, take a step back to an easier task or change the approach of your teaching to make the student successful. If you continue with a method that is not working, then child will not benefit.

4 TEACHING BASICS

Although many techniques are needed to teach students, a few items have proven to help in the process of educating students with autism. These items are in the graph below:

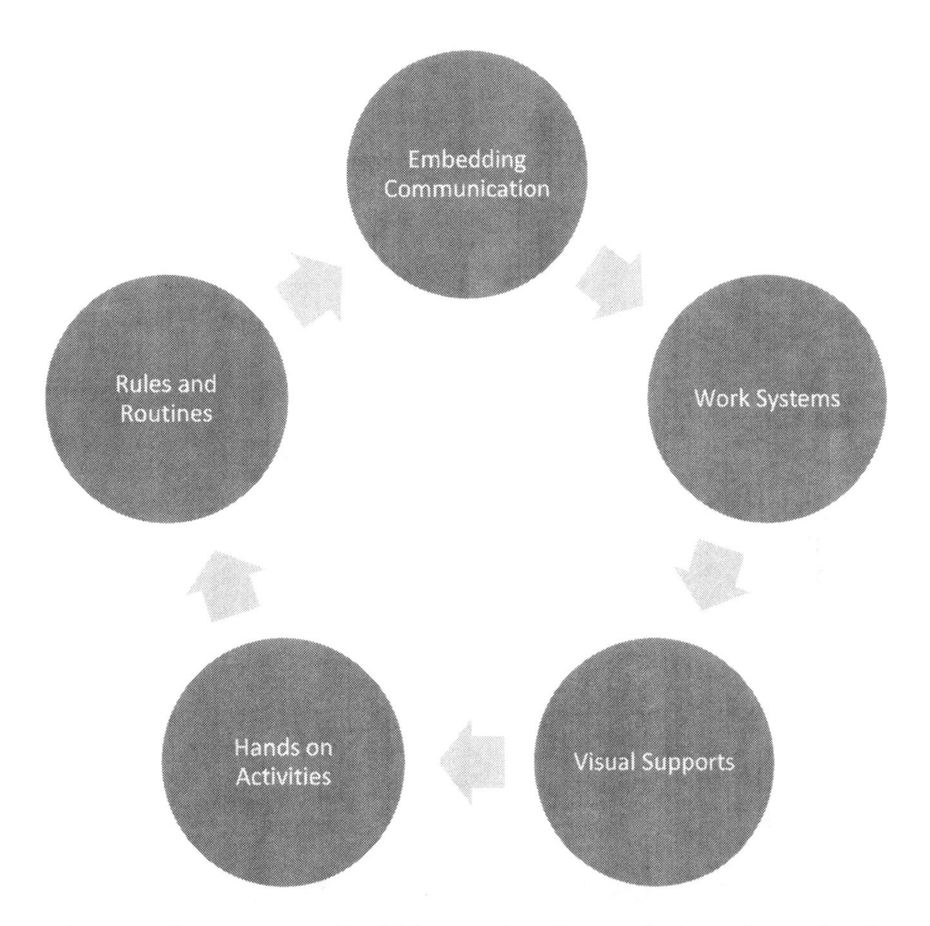

Structuring work systems, clarifying rules & routines, using visual supports, planning hands-on activities and embedding communication are all important techniques on their own. However, if the techniques are combined, it could mean greater gains for the individual with whom you are working.

????????????WHAT DO YOU THINK????????????

USE THE BLANK SPACES TO FINISH THE SENTENCES.

Rules are important because...

I can embed communication...

Some routines I would like my student to learn are...

Some visual supports I plan to use are...

Teaching Basics Explained...

WORK SYSTEMS -

Work systems are an organized way to let students clearly know what work is to be done, how much of it is to be done and when the work will be finished. This is done through visual cues such as checklists, picture schedules or setting up/modifying the work task ahead of time to show the student this information before they are expected to do the work. After completing work tasks, the students generally need a specific place to store their finished work. Many people believe in teaching the student to perform tasks in a left to right fashion because that is the way that we read.

RULES and ROUTINES -

Having a limited number of positively stated rules that are presented in writing or in picture form can be helpful. Having routines that are consistent and highly structured is a great teaching technique.

VISUAL SUPPORTS -

Visual supports include any visual item that helps a child to understand or express language. They include, but are not limited to photo icons, calendars, schedules, topic boards, single icons, written lists, written words, logos, and more. Visual schedules which are made to fit the specific needs of the students can be useful. Visual supports at mealtimes can be used to help students ask for food and materials. To do this, try having either food logos, wrappers, actual food items, photos or picture icons of the food that they can choose from. Have them point to, give you, or tell you, the item before consuming it. At first, you may find that some students may protest. If you are consistent during mealtimes, they will eventually learn to use a more symbolic form of communication whether it be handing a picture icon, signing or using words. Visual supports for routine daily living skills activities may help as well. For example, a set of pictures showing the steps in washing their hands or getting ready for class may help keep some students focused. Lastly, visual rules for behavior are helpful because the student may be more likely to look at the picture or written words, than to look at the adult. This is especially true when they are upset.

HANDS-ON ACTIVITIES -

Strive to have process-based activities where the process of doing the activity and putting forth effort in the activity is more important than the than what the product looks like. Encourage them to complete each of the steps of the process to help them learn the process correctly. It doesn't have to look perfect as long as the child worked hard to complete it.

EMBEDDING COMMUNICATION -

Embedding communication is necessary to make sure that students have a voice or a method of communication in each activity. It is important for educators to intentionally put in place ways for students to communicate such as words, pictures as communication, sign language, etc.

SO FAR…

SELF - ASSESSMENT

1. **What are 5 examples of characteristics of some individuals with autism?**

2. **What environmental adaptations might be useful in a school setting?**

3. **How might the color of a room affect a student with autism?**

4. **Why is collecting data and monitoring student progress important?**

5. **What is an example of a hands on lesson related to reading or math?**

STUDENT BEHAVIOR

The topic of understanding behavior is probably best understood in terms of reinforcement. People tend to do things that are reinforcing to them. The book *How to Set Up a Classroom for Students with Autism Second Edition*, explores this concept of reinforcement by explaining:

The concept of reinforcement in Applied Behavior Analysis is the most important concept to know when dealing with behavior. Reinforcers ***increase*** *the chance of a behavior occurring. Reinforcement is all about increasing the likelihood that a behavior will occur again. Sometimes this is done intentionally and planned. However, most times this is done inadvertently. ABA specialists, caretakers, and educators using ABA strategies, intentionally decide* ***when, what, and how often*** *to reinforce.*

However, to go a little further in to the concept, it will be useful to look at the definition of positive reinforcement. Positive reinforcement involves the presentation of items or actions that are done following a behavior, that increase the chance of a behavior happening again.

ONE EXAMPLE OF POSITIVE REINFORCEMENT:

(How to Set Up a Classroom for Students with Autism Second Edition, 2012)

A student who is motivated by the attention of adults, climbs on a table in the classroom. Each time he does this, the adult says "Timmy get down. You know better than that." Timmy's climbing continues, and even increases in numbers.

This is an example of positive reinforcement because after the target behavior (climbing) occurred, a stimulus was presented (the words "Timmy get down you know better than that.") That stimulus (the words "Timmy get down you know better than that.") increased the likelihood of the target behavior (climbing) happening again. As long as the student who is looking for attention, receives the attention, the behavior will increase.

In addition to learning about positive reinforcement, we should also look at the concept of negative reinforcement. Negative reinforcement involves the removal of items or actions that are taken away following a behavior, that increase the chance of a behavior happening again.

ONE EXAMPLE OF NEGATIVE REINFORCEMENT:

(How to Set Up a Classroom for Students with Autism Second Edition, 2012)

A student who is motivated by escape/avoiding a work activity, throws several items from his desk to the floor after being asked to complete his work. The teacher chastises the student and tells him that he has to go to the "time out area." The student stays in the timeout area for the several minutes and comes back to the work area. The target behavior occurs again (throwing items). The student is sent back to the time out area. The teacher complains that the behavior is not getting any better.

This is an example of negative reinforcement because after the target behavior (throwing items from the desk) occurred, a stimulus was taken away (work), increasing the likelihood of the behavior (throwing items) happening again. As long as the behavior results in the removal of work, the student whose motivation is to avoid/escape work, will continue the behavior.

What people find reinforcing is influenced by several factors. Some of the key factors are the immediacy of the reinforcement, the amount access the student has to the reinforcement prior to you offering it to them and the connection between the behavior and the reinforcement. The official terms for this are immediacy, establishing operations, and contingency.

FACTORS INFLUENCING REINFORCEMENT:

(Sources: How to Set Up a Classroom for Students with Autism Second Edition, 2012 & Behavior Modification: Principles and Procedures, 1997)

IMMEDIACY- It is known that reinforcement has to occur immediately for some individuals to make the connection between their actions and the reinforcement or consequence. For example someone on a 2-year old cognitive level may not understand a reinforcement or consequence that is delivered 2 hours after the behavior occurred.

ESTABLISHING OPERATIONS- This is the idea that you can set up the situation to alter the effectiveness of the reinforcement. For example, satiation (unlimited access to the reinforcement) may cause a student not to want the reinforcement anymore since they have had unlimited access to it. On the other hand, deprivation (little access to the reinforcement) will make the student more likely to find the item reinforcing.

CONTINGENCY- Contingent Reinforcement makes a clear connection between the target behavior and the reinforcement. The reinforcement or consequence is given when the child does the behavior. Non-Contingent Reinforcement means giving access to a desire activity or item without or without the child engaging in a behavior. With non-contingent reinforcement, (the attention, escape, a break, tangible object or sensory input) is provided at regularly scheduled times, so that the child will not have to do an inappropriate behavior to get the reinforcement.

As the person who is working directly with the student, you may want to know how you can tell what is reinforcing to each student. What motivates the student to do the behavior? What is the root cause of the behavior? It would be great if we did always know, but most often, we have to watch and make our best guess. One thing we know for sure is that there is a function or reason for each behavior. Generally, there are four functions of behaviors or reasons why people behavior they way they do. Sometimes, people choose to add a few other options for functions, and that is fine. However, the following information will focus on the four most commonly identified functions. People tend to engage in a behavior because they usually find one of the following items reinforcing:

- **Escape/Avoidance of a Situation**
  (i.e. work, uncomfortable clothes, loud noises, touching water)
- **Gaining Attention**
  (i.e. attention from the adult, attention from another student)
- **Gaining a Access to a Tangible Item**
  (i.e. getting access to foods, toys, books, teacher's materials)
- **Sensory Input**
  (i.e. spinning items, putting items in mouth, smelling things)

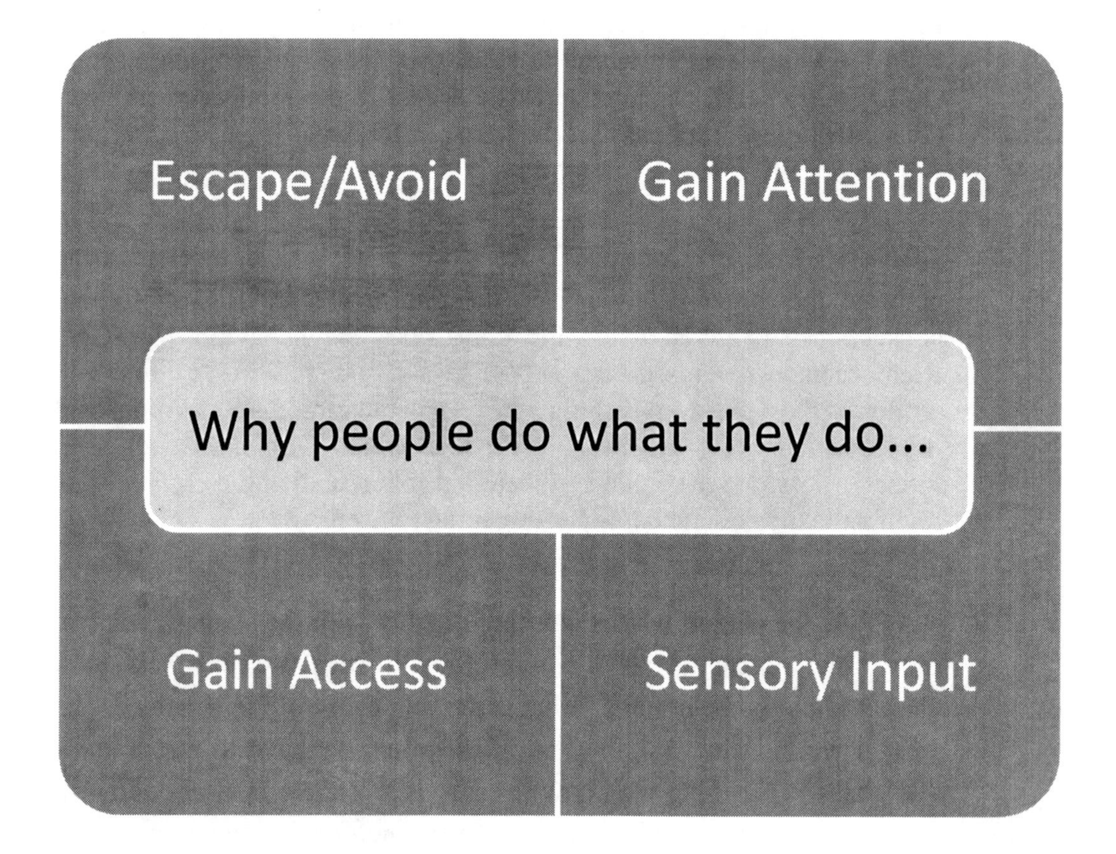

There are a few ways to find out the function. The most useful way is to take data and analyze the data. Also, there are some motivation assessments out there which will ask a series of questions and have you tally the answers to provide a pretty good prediction of the motivation or function of the behavior. We are going to examine some observational items you can look for to help in the process of figuring out the function for a behavior. The chart below provides some indicators that the person might show you for each function. (This is not an exhaustive list, as there are many other indicators for each function.)

IDENTIFYING THE REASONS FOR SOME BEHAVIORS

ESCAPE FUNCTION

Some indicators of escape/avoidance reinforcement are:

- The individual does the behavior when a task is presented.
- The individual does the behavior when a new activity begins.
- The individual does the behavior when something ***they*** view as aversive is presented.
- The individual does the behavior when an activity ***they*** view as aversive is presented
- The behavior ends when the student is allowed to leave the activity.

GAIN ATTENTION FUNCTION

Some indicators of attention gained reinforcement are:

- Attention (words, eye contact, body language) from the adult usually follows the behavior.
- The individual looks at or approaches a caregiver before engaging in the behavior.
- The individual smiles just before engaging in the behavior.

GAIN ACCESS TO TANGIBLE ITEM FUNCTION

Some indicators of access to a tangible item reinforcement are:

- The individual's behavior ends when given the item or activity.
- The individual asks for or requests the item.
- The individual's behaviors occur after it is clear that they cannot have the item they want.
- The individual's behavior occurs when the item is not presented fast enough.

GAIN SENSORY INPUT FUNCTION

Some indicators of sensory reinforcement are:

- The individual would do the behavior even when other people are out of the room.
- The individual appears to be enjoying the behavior, not aware of others around them, not being presented with a work activity, and not attempting to gain access to something.
- The individual appears to be doing the behavior because they need sensory input (ex. Pushing up against others, mouthing objects, squeezing others, banging tables, hands in ears, rolling on the floor, pacing around the room, getting up out of seat, etc.)

Once you know, or think you know, the function for the behavior, you can begin to stop reinforcing the child when they perform an inappropriate behavior. Consequently, you can purposefully reinforce them when they are performing appropriate behaviors. For the child that wants attention, this may mean providing attention when they are doing the correct thing and stopping all verbal attention when they are doing the inappropriate behavior. For the child who wants to escape/avoid a situation, this means not letting the inappropriate behavior get them out of doing the task. Additionally, for the child who wants to escape/avoid, you will need to build a break into the activity, help reduce the sensory input they are experiencing, or teach them a way to request a break instead of misbehaving. For the child who wants to gain access to an item, you can teach them how to properly request the item using words, pictures or sign language. Finally, for the child who is doing a behavior to get sensory input, you can try to see if there is another way for them to gain the same type of input without them doing the inappropriate behavior.

TEACH BEHAVIORS TO TAKE THE PLACE OF THE PROBLEM BEHAVIORS:

Think about what it is that you want the student to do. Teach them how to do that skill. For example, do you want them to request a break instead of just jumping up? Teach them another behavior or another way to get the same outcome. This way, they can do the appropriate skill instead of doing the problem behavior.

DRI (Differential Reinforcement of Incompatible Behaviors)- Provide reinforcement for a behavior that cannot happen at the same time as the problem behavior; ignore or block the problem behavior. (Ex. Holding something with 2 hands instead of hitting.)

DRA (Differential Reinforcement of Alternative Behaviors)- Provide reinforcement for an alternate behavior, but ignore or block the problem behavior. (Ex. Using a picture card to request a break instead of crying.)

DRO (Differential Reinforcement of Other Behaviors)- Provide reinforcement for a specific time period where the student does not do the problem behavior. (Ex. Student gets a piece of pretzel for each 1 minute without getting up out of seat.)

DRL (Differential Reinforcement of Other Behaviors)- Eliminate the frequency but not the behavior itself, by only reinforcing the behavior a set number of times per day. (Ex. Only answer the student's questions about dinosaurs 3 times per day, instead of 30.)

6 STOPPING BEHAVIORS BEFORE THEY START

Antecedent Based Interventions can eliminate many problem behaviors before they start. Antecedents refer to any events that happen before the behavior. The idea is that you change the antecedent so that the behavior does not happen in the first place. Having appropriate supports and strategies in place can greatly help get the student to do the right thing. These antecedent based strategies should be put in place to avoid challenging behaviors. The website www.autisminternetmodules.org provides free training about this topic and other topics. According to their website, antecedent based interventions include some of the following items, but are not limited to:

- planning appropriate lessons
- setting up the classroom specifically to meet the needs of students with autism
- providing students with visual supports
- giving students warnings when activities will end or new activities will begin
- changing the schedule or routine to fit the needs of the student
- giving students personalized schedules
- structuring the student's time and having a specific plan for what they will do during each portion of the school day
- reducing long periods of wait time
- using highly preferred items and highly preferred activities to increase interest
- providing communication systems for students to express wants and needs
- providing sensory input before an interfering behavior occurs

While planning and environmental arrangement help solve some problems, there are some challenging behaviors that may require even more techniques from the adult. Once a behavior begins, de-escalating the behavior is a needed quality for a 1:1 assistant for an individual with autism. De-escalating techniques are those things that you intentionally do to calm the student and those things you do to try to stop the behavior from getting more out of control. Many people have to train themselves to respond in this way. It is not the first way most people respond when dealing with a crisis situation. However, if you teach yourself to implement some of these strategies, you may find that you have decreased the magnitude of some behaviors before they get

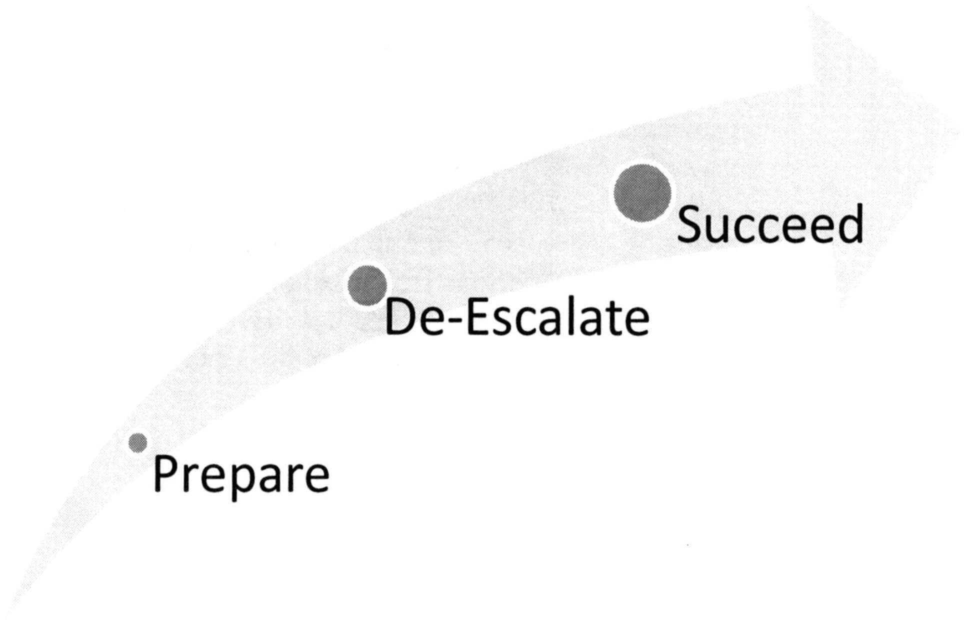

Succeed

De-Escalate

Prepare

completely out of control. De-escalating techniques during the beginning stages of a challenging behavior include some of the following.

De-Escalating Techniques and Strategies

www.autismclassroom.com

- Plan ahead and arrange the setting to avoid behaviors
- Be the person who helps them learn to control themselves; do not aim to control them
- Pay attention to the student's non-verbal language showing that a behavior might begin
- Stay calm and quiet; do not mention the inappropriate behavior
- Stop talking or use very, very few words
- Stop giving commands and demands; avoid threats
- Ask others around you to stop talking or use very, very few words
- Use sign language, written words on paper or picture icons to give directions
- Use neutral body language (relaxed arms, relaxed facial expressions, comfortable distance away, if possible)
- Move back away and give them some space, if possible
- Turn the lights down
- Turn the background noise off
- Remove the audience (Having other students watching can cause behaviors to increase. Having other adults watching and adding their input could interfere with the behavior plan.)
- Tell the adults whether or not you need assistance with the student by stating "Thank you for your offer to help, but I will be fine with the student right now" or "I need some help. Could you please, without talking to him/her, help me to (fill in the blank)."
- Empathize. Think about how they might be feeling and why. State that you empathize "I know that sound hurts your ears."
- Make clear statements about what should happen next using very little language (ex. "Time for math class.)
- Provide choices (ex "Do you want to walk to class or skip to class? Do you want the red or blue pencil to complete your work?")
- Keep the student safe
- Ask the school system if they can offer you training in Crisis Intervention/Prevention

DE-ESCALATION PLAN

The Challenging Behavior: Crying during the reading lesson that usually results in hitting and arching back to get out of seat.

Possible Reason for the Behavior: Trying to avoid the work task during reading.

Antecedent Changes I Could Make:

1. Use visual cues to show how much work is to be done and when it will end.
2. Have a fun item waiting to play with after the work is done.
3. Make the reading activity fun.
4. Have the student choose the book.

De-Escalation Techniques I Could Use:

1. Stay calm.
2. Use very little talking to address the situation.
3. Provide choices by asking which color pencil they want to use or which paper to use.
4. Use picture cues to give directions instead of words.

Behaviors I Could Teach to Take the Place of the Challenging Behaviors:

1. How to ask for a break.
2. How to read a personalized schedule.
3. How to say, use sign language or pictures to say "I don't like this."
4. How to say, use sign language or pictures to say "I want to read a different book."

Supports Needed: Picture icons, visual cues, fun items the student likes, various book choices

DE-ESCALATION PLAN

The Challenging Behavior:

Possible Reason for the Behavior:

Antecedent Changes I Could Make:

1.
2.
3.
4.

De-Escalation Techniques I Could Use:

1.
2.
3.
4.

Behaviors I Could Teach to Take the Place of the Challenging Behaviors:

1.
2.
3.
4.

Supports Needed:

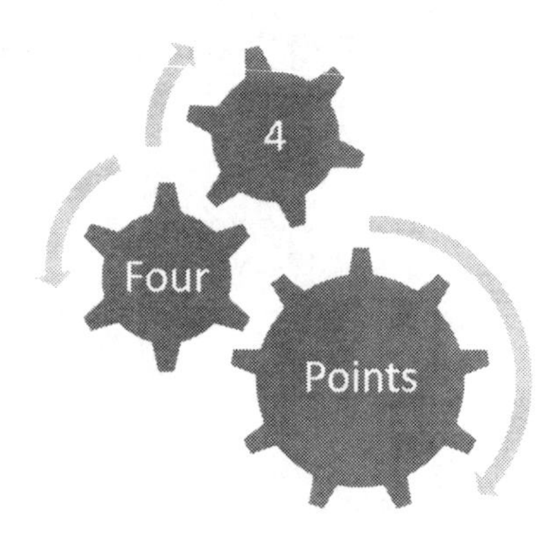

WHAT IS THIS?

Antecedent Based Interventions are strategies you put into place before a behavior occurs to try to stop the trigger or triggers for the behavior.

WHAT DOES THIS MEAN?

It means that you think about what you can do to prevent the behaviors instead of just reacting to behaviors. You set up the environment, the lessons and the supports to try to stop the behavior from happening in the first place.

WHY IS THIS IMPORTANT TO ME?

If you can learn to eliminate behaviors and reduce behaviors, there will be more time for instruction and you will experience less stress.

WHY IS THIS IMPORTANT TO THE STUDENT?

If students are having less behavior challenges, they will be less stressed in the school setting. This will help them to maximize their ability to learn.

7 USING A VISUAL SYSTEM

Visual systems are essential because we know that students with autism are often visual learners. Many individuals learn better by seeing what we mean than by hearing what we say. This is where visual systems can come into play and make communication between you the individual you are working with more effective. Visual systems are relevant to students in the areas of time management, routines, work tasks and reinforcement.

WHY WOULD A VISUAL SYSTEM BE NEEDED?

- ✓ *The student has trouble completing routines.*
- ✓ *The student has trouble following directions.*
- ✓ *The student is easily distracted.*
- ✓ *The student takes things from others.*
- ✓ *The student won't complete work tasks.*
- ✓ *The student does not want to leave their favorite activity without a protest.*

Visual systems can be created in a variety of ways. It will be up to you to decide which type of system will be most helpful for the individual you are working with. In many cases, it may be up to you to create these systems too. They will make your day and the student's day run much smoother once they get the hang of it. Examples of some of these items can be found by doing a search engine image search of the term "visual supports autism." The following page gives a few ideas on how to include some visual supports throughout the day.

Ideas for Including Visual Systems...

VISUAL SYSTEMS FOR TIME MANAGEMENT -

- Visual schedules of the day's events
- Visual schedules of the expectations in each activity
- Sand timers, kitchen egg timers, commercially bought "Time Timers"
- Count down board with detachable numbers 5-4-3-2-1-finished
- Verbal warnings that an activity is almost finished
- Visual warnings that an activity is almost finished (Picture of "1 more minute")
- Visual turn taking board to tell when a turn is up
- Sign Language
- "First, Then" Board to show what activity will be next
- Visual monthly calendar to see when special activities will occur

VISUAL SYSTEMS FOR ROUTINES -

- Picture schedules showing how to complete the routine (ex. Hand-washing)
- Checklists for organizing steps in a routine
- Photo examples of how the task is done
- Photo examples of how chores are completed
- Social Stories ™ for teaching routines
- Color code bins for various materials and activities
- Color code student belongings

VISUAL SYSTEMS WORK TASKS -

- Should be organized in a way to let students clearly know what work is to be done, how much of it is to be done and when the work will be finished (TEACCH.com)
- Must be set up and adjusted ahead of time to make the task VERY clear
- Usually organized in a left to right or top to bottom fashion and include a specific place to store their finished work
- Do not continuously give task after task without providing a pre-scheduled break or telling the student how much work is to be completed
- Break the tasks into smaller "chunks" with short break times (playing with a break item in the seat) if the student has trouble focusing for long periods of time

REINFORCEMENT -

- "First, Then" Board to show what fun activity will be after the work activity
- Token boards that the student can earn something once they get 3 or 5 tokens
- Puzzle "token board" where a picture of the item the student is working for is enlarged then cut into 3 or 4 pieces and they can earn a piece at a time, once it is all back together, they get the item
- Self-Monitoring Checklist where the student checks if they followed directions

8 TECHNOLOGY

Technology use in education is at an all time high. As a 1:1 special educator, you will find yourself using technology to teach students. Here are a few apps and websites that may be useful.

For Kids

Websites

starfall.com
pbskids.org
nickjr.com
kids.nationalgeographic.com

Apps

More Cookies! (Maverick Software LLC)
Conversation Builder (Mobile Ed Tools)
Elmo Monster Maker (Sesame Street)
Tozzle (Nodeflexion.com)

For Teens

Websites

CoolMath4Kids.com
Lego.com
MakeMeGenius.com
more.starfall.com

Apps

Manners (Conover Company)
Hidden Curriculum (AAPC)
Dexteria-Fine Motor (Binary Labs)
Cut the Rope HD Lite (Chillingo Ltd)

Many schools are investing in iPads™, and other tablets for students to use. One area people are having difficulty with is figuring out how to incorporate the apps into the curriculum and into the lessons. AutismClassroom.com's book *Lesson Ideas and Activities for Young Children with Autism and Related Special Needs* answers this question with a chapter dedicated to incorporating apps into lessons. A few examples are below.

USING IPAD and IPHONE APPS IN LESSONS FOR YOUNGER STUDENTS

(Source: *Lesson Ideas and Activities for Young Children with Autism & Related Special Needs, S. B. Linton)*

Joint Attention/Attending to the Same Activity

- **Balloons (Chudigi Software, $0.99)**- Use this app first, then play a game of blowing up, then deflating balloons.
- **Pocket Piano HD (Better Day Wireless, Free)**- Discuss or hum familiar tunes then play a tune that is familiar. Press anywhere on the screen to make a sound.

Imitation Skills/Matching

- **Animal Memory Match (Imagam.com, $0.99)**- Read a story about the animals in the app, then have students play the matching game about animals.
- **Talking Roby Celik the Robot for iPad (Outfit7, Free)**- Give students vocabulary words on a sentence strip or on paper. Have students type in (give assistance when needed) the word onto the robot's screen. Listen to the robot repeat what is typed.

Self- Help

- **ASD Timer (In the Round Studios, $2.99)**- Use this app with students who may be having a difficult time giving up a turn. Emphasize the visual timer when their turn is almost over.
- **First/Then Visual Schedule (Good Karma Applications, Inc., $9.99)**- Use this app during difficult transition to visually show the student the order of events for the immediate future.

Play Skills

- **Glow Hockey 2 for iPad Free (Natenai Ariyatrakool, Free)**- Divide the students into groups. Have one group work in the play area using a real hockey puck and hockey stick, the second group at a small table learning the vocabulary terms about hockey and the third group taking turns using the air hockey app.
- **Color My Name (Girl's World Pty. Ltd, $1.99)**- This app is perfect for an "All About Me" unit. Use it 1:1 with a student to have them design an art project based around their first name.

Vocabulary/Literacy

- **Learning Game - Little Matchups Fruits (GrasshopperApps.com, $0.99)**- If teaching a lesson on "inside" and "outside" you can customize this game to choose the fruits you want to focus on. Each match has you match the inside of the fruit to its full, uncut counterpart.
- **Sightwords by PhotoTouch (GrasshopperApps.com, Free)**- Use vocabulary words from your story of the day to customize this app to created an in app spelling game.

The kids, however, are not the only ones who can benefit from smart phone and tablet apps. There are many apps that make teaching easier as well. This list includes:

- Autism Classroom
- Kindergarten.com apps
- Teens with Autism and Developmental Disabilities
- Tally Counter
- Percentally
- Numbers
- Touch Autism

As a 1:1 you will need to familiar yourself with websites can help you with teaching students who have special needs. A few websites that can help are:

- BoardMakerShare.com
- AutismClassroom.com
- AutismIntenetModules.org
- Pete's Power Point Station (pppst.com)
- PreschoolPrintables.com
- CindysAutisticSupport.com/printables.html
- AutismTeachingStrategies.com/our-how-to-videos-2/

SO FAR...

SELF - ASSESSMENT

1. **What does it mean to reinforce something?**

2. **Are most people aware that they are reinforcing behaviors? Explain why.**

3. **List 3 de-escalation techniques you would like to practice.**

4. **What are four common reasons for behaviors?**

5. **What is DRO?**

SOCIAL SKILLS and PLAY SKILLS

Social skills are key elements to learning. Individuals with autism need instruction in the area of increasing social skills. This means you will have to teach various social skills as well as play skills, since they do not come naturally for many individuals with autism. However, with instruction, skills can increase. Instruction of social skills and play skills should be planned, purposeful and meaningful. The goal should be to increase the student's ability level in some of the areas listed below.

Joint Attention- *The ability to watch others and pay attention to the same thing at the same time with others.* Many children with autism have difficulty with this skill. You will have to first start paying attention to things they are interested in so that you can build a bond with them. Begin by noticing what they like or asking their parents what they like and then commenting on that in front of the student. Sometimes just talking about an episode of their favorite cartoon may be enough to have them pay attention to you.

Imitation- *The ability to copy others actions.* Most people learn this way, by watching what others do, but individuals with autism who are missing this piece are missing a key part of learning. Most often, at the beginning of teaching this skill, you can imitate some of the person's actions or you can physically guide them to do the correct imitation, then reinforce immediately with an item they really like. By reinforcing, you hope to build a connection between them imitating you and the fun reward that follows.

Imaginative Play- *The ability to play using imagination.* This skill is difficult for some individuals because some individuals with autism tend to like to deal in facts and non-fiction. Also, some children develop rote play patterns where they tend to do the same actions over and over with a toy or game.

Interacting with Others- *The skill of taking turns, communicating and playing with another person.* Communicating with others, following group directions, taking turns, is a much needed skill in a school setting. Adults must find ways and create lessons that actively teach these skills to students who need them.

STRATEGIES FOR TEACHING PLAY SKILLS AND SOCIAL SKILLS

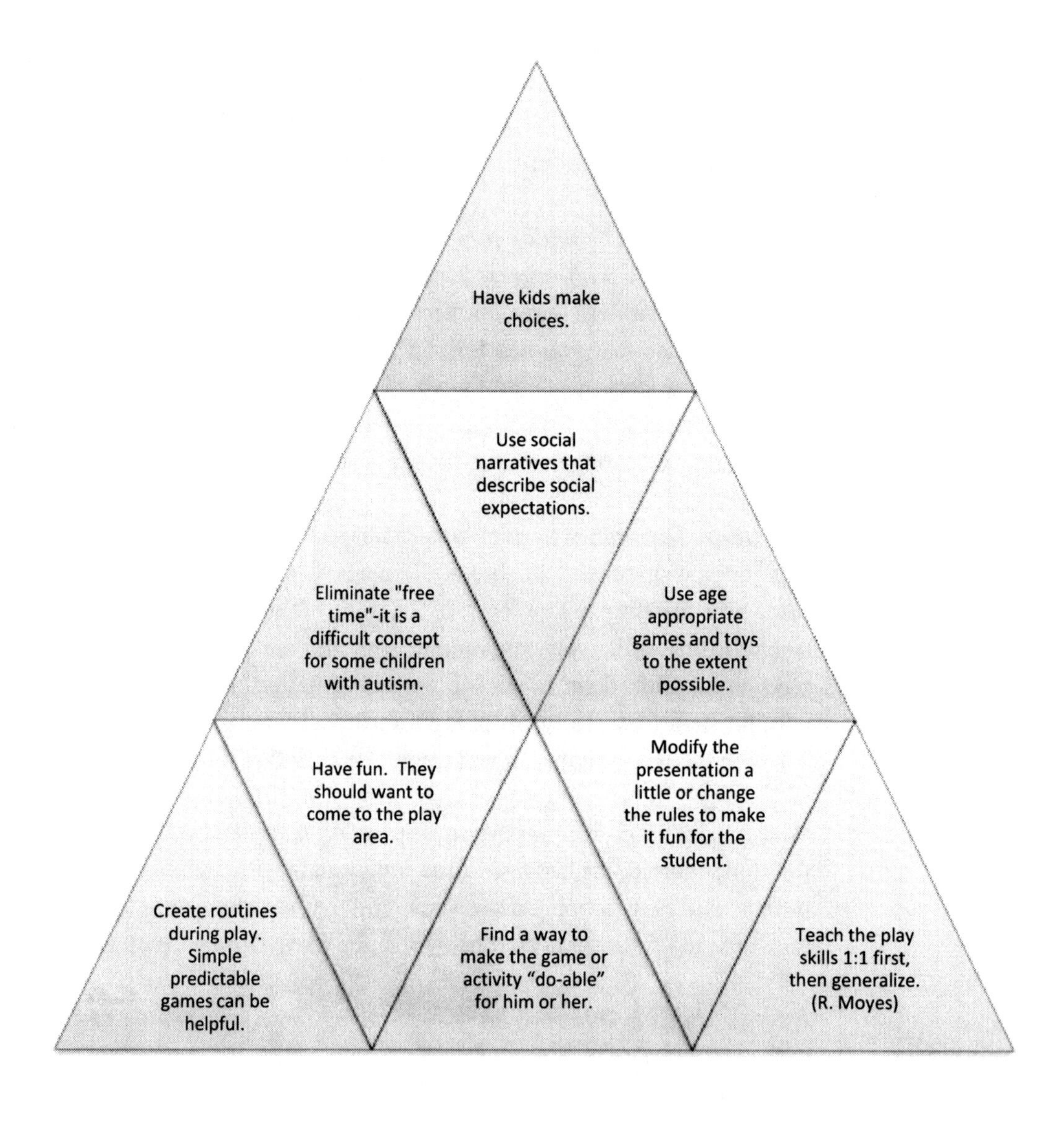

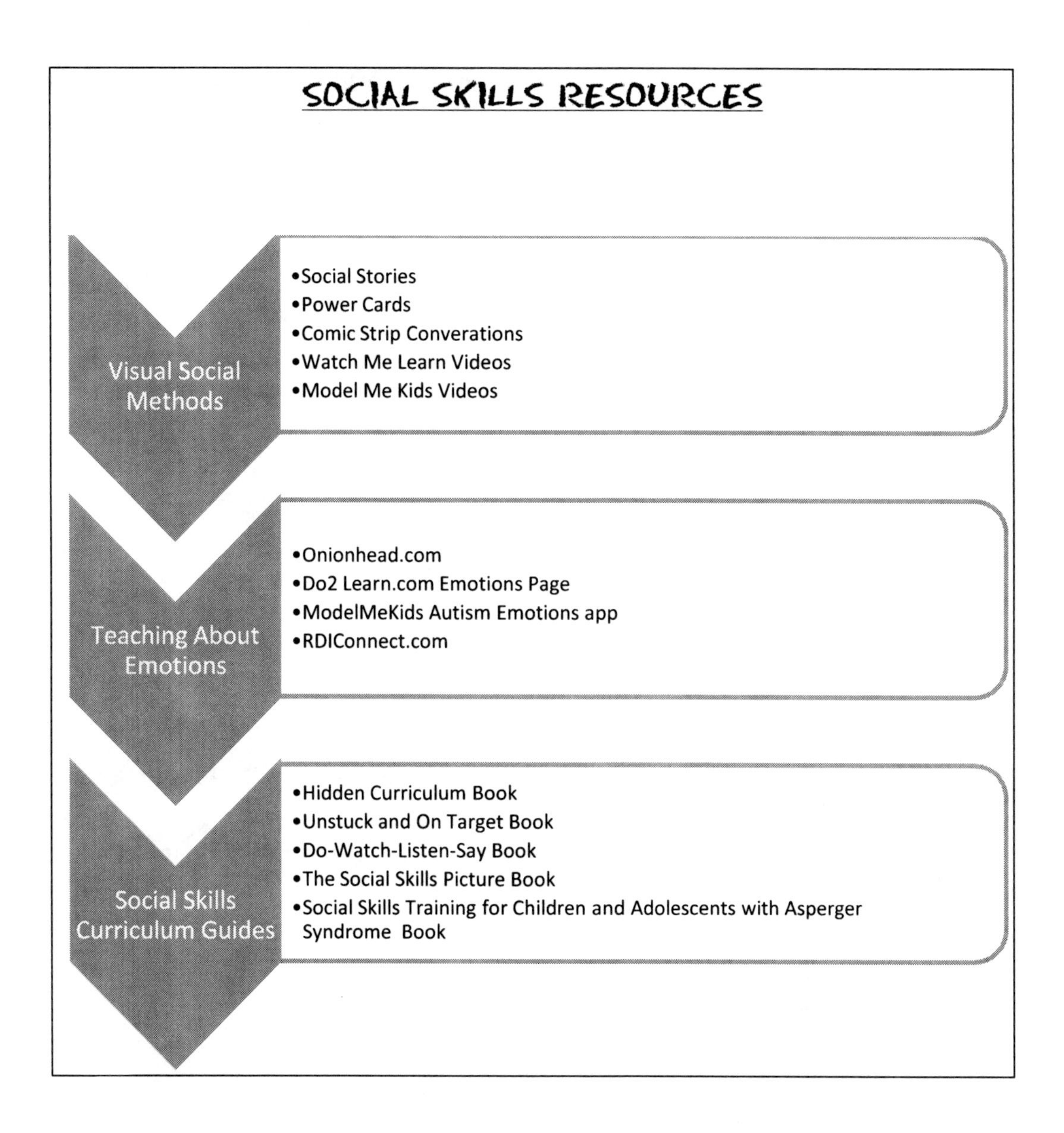

Books, websites and videos like those listed above are extremely useful when teaching social skills. Even with those supports, there must be time dedicated to using these items. There are a few techniques for organizing the play and social skills instructional time that may be helpful. These techniques are listed on the following page.

ORGANIZING THE TEACHING SETTING FOR PLAY INSTRUCTION

- Set aside specific time to teach play skills and social skills.
- Store items in containers and make students ask for the items.
- Set up a situation where they need to ask for it, use sign language or use a picture to request an item; When you see that they are interested, you wait to see if they will ask, if they don't then you say "What do you want?" or "What's this?"
- Occasionally take the toy away or stop the activity to encourage the student to ask for "more" or to request the toy again.
- Label items to encourage communication.
- Follow their lead in the beginning stages.
- Create boundaries by using chairs and tables in the play area for the student and a peer to sit at.
- Use furniture to block off a specific area for play time or social skills time.
- Do not limit play to only toys, use items the child likes to build your interactions.
- Set a timer if needed.
- Do not "test" during play (Ex. "What color is it?")
- Use more comments instead of questions.
- Over exaggerate your expressions.
- Be silly.
- Have fun.

10 SENSORY DIFFERENCES

Our sensory system helps us to gain information from the environment. Individuals with autism who can tell us what they feel have described their sensory systems as being either over reactive or under reactive. At times, sensory issues can make it hard for an individual with autism to concentrate or to tolerate a particular smell, sound or sight. They may use a behavior use to avoid that smell, sound or sight. When this happens, sometimes the adult sees this as misbehavior, when in fact, there may be a sensory issue they are trying to avoid. If this appears to be the case, it is a good idea to talk with the Occupational Therapist in your school building to get professional advice regarding sensory issues. Sometimes the Occupational Therapist will observe the student and suggest a sensory diet. A sensory diet is a planned and scheduled activity program that an Occupational Therapist develops to help a person become more self-regulated; it consists of multi-sensory experiences that a person seeks each day to satisfy their sensory appetite (Kranowitz, 1998). The goal of a sensory diet is to provide the sensory input that the student craves on a regular and planned basis to help keep the student functioning at his or her best. The sensory diet is individualized and based on the needs and preferences of that particular student. You may wonder if the student you work with has a sensory difference. The following pages have information from the book The Out of Sync Child by Carol Stock Kranowitz (1998). The book is about sensory differences.

THE SENSES

TOUCH

SIGHT

TASTE

HEARING

SMELL

PROPRIOCEPTIVE

VESTIBULAR

SENSORY AREAS and POSSIBLE INDICATORS OF A SENSORY DIFFERENCE

TOUCH

Fearful, anxious or aggressive when touched lightly or unexpectedly

Becomes afraid when touched from behind or by someone or something they are not able to see

Avoids or dislikes playing in sand, mud, water, glue, etc.

Will not wear clothes with certain textures

Picky eater

Seeks out touch, appears to need to touch everything and everyone

Is not aware of being touched or bumped

Puts objects in mouth often

SIGHT

Easily distracted by visual stimuli in the room (ex. movement, decoration, toys, doorways)

Does not make or makes limited eye contact

Notices details or patterns and not the larger picture

Difficulty finding differences in pictures, words, symbols or objects

TASTE

Picky eater

Prefers to eat hot or cold foods

Puts objects in mouth often

Drools a lot

HEARING

Distracted by sounds that do not typically affect others (ex. humming of lights or refrigerators, fans or clocks)

Startled by loud or unexpected sounds

Might put hands over ears

Does not answer when name is called

Listens to excessively loud music or TV

SMELL

Unusual response to smells which don't bother others

May not eat certain foods due to smell

Irritated by strong scents

Difficulty discriminating unpleasant odors

Fails to pay attention to unpleasant odors

PROPRIOCEPTIVE

Likes jumping and crashing activities

Enjoys being wrapped tight in weighted blankets

May hit, bump or push others often

Uses too little or too much force with objects

Difficulty catching self if falling

VESTIBULAR

Avoids moving playground equipment

Afraid of having feet leave the ground

Does not like rapid or rotating movement

Constantly moving

Could spin for hours & does not appear dizzy

Seeks out fast, spinning and intense movement

BOOKS ABOUT SENSORY DIFFERENCES

The Out of Sync Child
The Out of Sync Child Has Fun
Raising a Sensory Smart Kid
Growing an In-Sync Child
Sensational Kids

WEBSITES ABOUT SENSORY DIFFERENCES

www.sensory-processing-disorder.com

www.spdfoundation.net

www.sensoryprocessingmadesimple.com

SENSORY RELATED APPS

Soundythingie app
Rain Stick app
Magic Window Living Pictures app
Brainworks app
P.O.V. Spatial Skills Development app

11 PROFESSIONAL EXPECTATIONS

Working in the professional setting requires you to know the professional expectations. Too often, 1:1 assistants are asked to work with a student without being given any information, workshops or training about the needs of the student or the rules of the building. However, there are some important things to know about working in an educational setting. For one, it will be important to find out what the job expectations are. Many students do require behavioral support, but others require personal care as well. This personal care and support may be part of their educational plan and is often critical to their growth and progress. Also, it is important to remember that the student's individualized education program (IEP) is a legal written agreement between the parents and the school system and must be implemented according to what it says on it. Educators are bound by law to do what is on the IEP.

Laws also play a role in our everyday interactions with students. At the beginning of the school year, schools are required to have a training or workshop about the laws concerning child abuse and child neglect. If you have not had this training, ask an administrator about it. In the end, the most important rule of interacting with the child is to treat them with respect. This includes the way you talk to the student and the way you talk about the student. If you have a concern about the student's behavior or another personal matter related to that student, it would be best to discuss it after school or at a time when students are not around. That is a discussion for adults and not appropriate to do in front of the students. Confidentially is needed because student's information and situations are extremely sensitive and are not for public knowledge. When you are talking to the student, be sure to use respectful references, encouraging words, a calm voice and the "golden rule" when interacting.

PEOPLE FIRST LANGUAGE

People first language is a way to show respect for individuals by emphasizing their humanity first.

"People-First Language emphasizes the person, not the disability. By placing the person first, the disability is no longer the primary, defining characteristic of an individual, but one of several aspects of the whole person. People-First Language is an objective way of acknowledging, communicating, and reporting on disabilities. It eliminates generalizations and stereotypes, by focusing on the person rather than the disability. People-First Language emphasizes the person, not the disability. By placing the person first, the disability is no longer the primary, defining characteristic of an individual, but one of several aspects of the whole person. People-First Language is an objective way of acknowledging, communicating, and reporting on disabilities. It eliminates generalizations and stereotypes, by focusing on the person rather than the disability." (TheArc.org)

Example: Say "a person with an intellectual disability," "people with autism" or "a person who is hard of hearing."

Another area often overlooked related to professional expectations is the idea of collaboration. You will be expected to communicate with many people who also work with the student. When doing so, keep in mind the skill of being objective. Being objective includes stating information in facts, not opinions. For example, if a student is having a "tantrum," describe exactly what he is doing (hitting, kicking, yelling and sitting on the floor) instead of saying he was "out of control." If the student cannot tell you how they feel you could try to describe her actions like this, "She ***appeared*** to be upset, because she did these things…" This same objectivity is useful in interactions with adults. Just talk about the facts.

MY COLLABORATION STYLE

Think a little about your collaboration style. Use the chart below to write down your collaboration style in the blank spaces.

	Now…	In The Future…
My Communication Style		
My Teaching Style		
My Leadership Style		
My Argument Style		

PROFESSIONAL EXPECTATIONS TO THINK ABOUT

Be Discrete

- Don't make or accept personal calls during work hours.
- Don't make or accept text messages during work hours.
- Keep personal matters outside of the classroom.
- Avoid disscussions during instruction.
- Try to provide directions to the students in a whisper so that the other students will not be distracted.
- You do not have to say everything you are thinking.

Be Present

- Be on time.
- Call the princpal and classroom teacher if you will not be on time.
- Be present.
- Call the princpal and classroom teacher as soon as you know you will not be coming in to work the following day.
- Don't make or accept personal calls or texts during work hours.
- Don't wear headphones during work hours.
- Greet others by name.

Empower Yourself

- Share your talents. Let others know what skills you bring to the table.
- Join activities or committees within the school or school system.
- Do above and beyond what is asked.
- Volunteer to help with a school wide project to get to know other teachers and assistants within the entire building.
- Dress professionally. Avoid flipflops, tank tops and other casual clothing.

There are a few methods for communicating that can help with collaboration. Try to employ these methods listed below when interacting with

Don't Take Things Personally

- Try To See The Other Person's Point Of View
- Keep Calm
- Listen More Than You Talk
- Avoid Sarcasm
- Smile

co-workers, families and students. While doing so, best wishes on a happy, safe, productive school year.

NOTES:

RESOURCES

Books

Ingenmey, R., & Van Houten, R. (1991). Using time delay to promote spontaneous speech in an autistic child. Journal of Applied Behavior Analysis, 24, 591-596.

Linton, S. B. (2012). How to Set Up a Classroom for Students with Autism Second Edition. AutismClassroom.com

Linton, S. B. (2009). Lesson Ideas and Activities for Young Children with Autism & Related Special Needs: Activities, Apps & Lessons for Joint Attention, Imitation, Play, Social Skills & More AutismClassroom.com

Miltenberger, Raymond G. (1997). Behavior Modification: Principles and Procedures. Wadsworth.

Moyes, Rebecca (2002). Addressing Challenging Behaviors in High Functioning Autism and Asperger's Syndrome. London: Jessica Kingsley Publishers Ltd.

Noonan, M. J., & McCormick, L. (1993). Early intervention in natural environments: methods and procedures. Pacific Grove, CA: Brooks/Cole.

Stock Kranowitz, Carol (2006). The Out-of-Sync Child: Recognizing and Coping with Sensory Processing Disorder. Penguin Group (USA).

Websites

www.AutismClassroom.com

www.AutismInternetModules.org

www.Autism-Society.org

www.teacch.com

ABOUT THE AUTHOR:

S. B. Linton has worked with children with autism for over 15 years. She has a Master's Degree in Teaching Students with Severe Disabilities and a Graduate Certificate in Autism Spectrum Disorders. Linton is the author of other books: *How to Set Up a Classroom for Students with Autism Second Edition, How to Set Up a Work Area at Home for a Child with Autism,* and *Lesson Ideas and Activities for Young Children with Autism & Related Special Needs:Activities, Apps & Lessons for Joint Attention, Imitation, Play, Social Skills & More.* Linton is the owner of the AutismClassroom.com website, which provides autism information and materials for parents and educators. She currently works as an Autism Instructional Specialist and consults with school teams in matters related to teaching students with autism.

CPSIA information can be obtained at www.ICGtesting.com
Printed in the USA
LVOW09s2239090114

368772LV00006B/567/P